Attitude

Category: Business & Economics
©2017 Standard Copyright License
ISBN 978-1-105-22593-2
Author: Bob Oros

Description: Define what you want and go after it. Being aggressive means moving towards what you want with the right mental attitude and taking for granted that you will get it. You will have a clearly defined objective and you will be automatically moving toward it. Any problems or obstacles you encounter will be welcomed as opportunities.

Key words: attitude, attitude control

Table of Contents

What the Ben Franklin Sales Program will do for you 5
Ben Franklin's system 6
Achieve a 52% improvement 11
Attitude: 13
Why so many fail 16
Review your success 22
Goal setting – what's the point? 27
Fork in the road 33
Customers aren't buying 36
Tough time for a new rep 39
Running Scared 45
Attitude: Define what you want and go after it 49
    About the author Bob Oros (BobOros.com), ... 51

What the Ben Franklin Sales Program will do for you

Investing in the Ben Franklin Sales Program is like hiring 13 powerful coaching sessions that will increase every skill necessary for generating business. Once you experience the seemingly effortless improvement you will understand why there is a picture of Ben Franklin on every 100-dollar bill.

You will learn how to improve relationships, improve management skills, be more productive, generate more customers, negotiate better contracts, open new accounts, earn more profits and create more sales! Results most people only dream about! If you are a sales professional or an entrepreneur this is the perfect program to boost your sales and increase your profits.

Ben Franklin's system

In our fast-paced business and personal life today it has become increasingly difficult to set aside time for self-development and improving your skills. With every spare minute taken up by reading blogs, logging on to Facebook, following people on Twitter, responding to text messages and emails and constantly talking on your cell phone, there seems to be little, if any, time left for learning new skills. Even the quiet time behind the wheel of your car is no longer available with satellite radio and cell phone coverage in every corner of the country.

Even though this seems like a new problem, distractions have been around forever. Two hundred years ago a man by the name of Ben Franklin had the same problem. He concluded that it was not a matter of distractions as much as a matter of focus. He set out to solve the problem and created the most effective system for self-improvement ever invented.

Ben Franklin gives credit for all his success and accomplishments to the implementation of this system for the success he sought after. Despite being born into a poor family and only receiving two years of formal schooling, Ben Franklin became a successful printer, scientist, musician, author and one of the founding fathers of the United States. Ben Franklin is considered to have been one of the most persuasive and successful people in the history of the United States. He was a very skilled salesperson, marketer, negotiator and copywriter. Skills that every business owner, professional person, manager and marketer should have.

In the year 1723, Ben Franklin, at the age of seventeen, arrived in Philadelphia without a penny to his name. At age 42, he retired, wealthy, the first self-made millionaire in the country. Few people, before or since have ever been as successful as Benjamin Franklin. He gave credit for his many inventions and business successes to his system for self-improvement he created when he was 20 years old.

The key to Franklin's success was his drive to constantly improve himself and accomplish his ambitions. In order to accomplish his goal, Franklin developed and committed himself to a personal improvement program that consisted of mastering 13 principles.

When he was seventy-nine years old, Benjamin Franklin wrote more about this idea than anything else that ever happened to him in his entire life. He felt that he owed all his success and happiness to this one thing. Franklin wrote: "I hope, therefore, that some of my descendants may follow the example and reap the benefit."

Since success is developed by performing small and seemingly insignificant acts, you can use this method by reading and putting into practice the 13 skills that will guarantee your success in sales with scientific certainty.

This program takes advantage of Franklin's system and applies it to improving your skills as a sales professional. This program will show you how to dominate your market by first dominating yourself. By focusing on the 13 skills that make up a highly effective and successful sales professional. As these skills are improved your results and sales increases will also show a dramatic improvement.

The goal of going through the program the first time is to increase each skill by only four percent. With the accomplishment of this small improvement in each skill or attitude your overall improvement will be 52%. Those are results most people only dream about. However, you can accomplish this by investing as little as 45 minutes once a week reading one book and then focusing on improving the single skill during the rest of the week.

The second week by reading the second book and focusing on that single skill during the week and so on until all 13 weeks are completed.

You can write the single word on the back of your business card and tape it to your dashboard as a reminder. You can put this one word on your smart phone as a reminder as well as on your email signature, your Facebook page or you can even have something worthwhile to tweet about. One word, one week, one skill, one "I am" statement, 4% improvement objective and your subconscious mind will receive the message through all the clutter and act on it.

After the first time through the process you can do as Ben Franklin suggests and go through the program a second, third and fourth time. Get your whole sales team on the same page at the same time and you will experience a whirlwind of new excitement and new business.
Or get a likeminded colleague and join forces with accountability and focus.

Achieve a 52% improvement

Using Franklin's scientific program for learning your objective is to improve 4% in each area over 13 weeks.

1. Attitude Define what you want and go after it.
2. Respect Earn respect-no more comfort zone.
3. Service Help customers build their business.
4. Urgency Be enthusiastic get things done now.
5. Confidence Remove restrictions and limitations.
6. Persistence Keep going and never give up.
7. Planning Get big results by setting big goals.
8. Questions Ask questions that make the sale.
9. Attention Get attention with irresistible offers.
10. Presenting Give reasons why they should buy.
11. Objections Remove every roadblock to the sale.
12. Closing Ask for the order and get paid.
13. Follow up Remove all hope for competitors.

For complete details visit www.BobOros.com

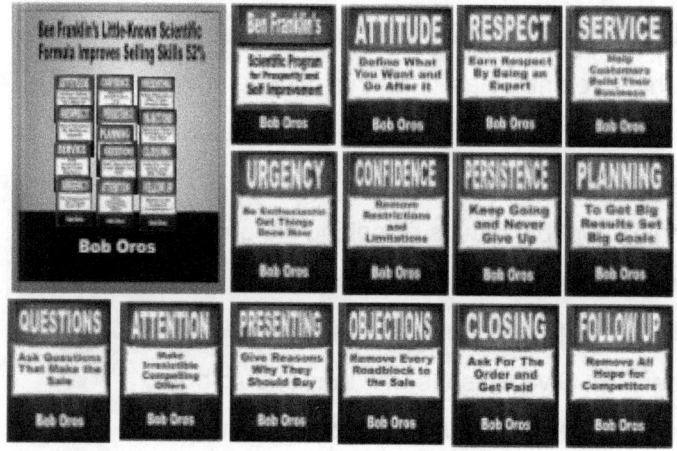

Attitude:
Define what you want and go after it

Death Valley

Death Valley, located within the Mojave Desert, received its name in 1849 during the California Gold Rush. It was named Death Valley by these Gold seekers who crossed the valley in search of their fortune because of the extreme heat.

The depth and shape of Death Valley influence its summer temperatures. The valley is a long, narrow basin 282 feet below sea level, yet is walled by high, steep mountain ranges. Summer nights provide little relief as overnight lows may only dip to 95°F. Moving masses of super-heated air blow through the valley creating extreme high temperatures.

The hottest temperature ever recorded in Death Valley was 134°F. The five consecutive day record was 129°F. In 1953 no rain was recorded for the whole year. In contrast to the extremes of summertime, winter and spring are very pleasant.

The California Gold Rush (1848 to 1859) was one of the most significant events in California history. It brought people from all over the United States and the world in search of gold. Rumors of gold in California had existed for years before the Gold Rush. But it wasn't until gold was discovered at Sutter's mill that the Gold Rush began.

It was very important that the travelers left early enough so not to get caught in the Sierra Mountains during the winter. This meant crossing Death Valley during the hottest time of the year - July.

They would pack a cooking stove, plates, cups, forks and knives. They would carry enough food and supplies for a 6-month journey. Food was usually bacon, ham, dried fruits, bread, flour, sugar, rice, molasses, butter, coffee and tea.

These gold seekers would also take tools for mining, farming and fixing the wagon as well as guns, ammunition, clothes and blankets. All of this had to be carried in a wagon about 9 feet long and 4 feet wide.

Think of the mind set these gold seekers must have had. Knowing you were going to have to walk for six months. Knowing that you would have to cross Death Valley during the hottest time of the year. What do you think their attitude was as they were facing these extreme elements? This was no casual commitment; this was a do-or-die definite decision.

This was a difficult trip. Many people died during the journey from illness and starvation. The main reason these people died was due to being poorly prepared. They didn't realize that you don't just strike out on a six-month journey without some thorough preparation.

Here's my question for you. Would you have made the trip? Could you maintain the kind of motivation necessary to keep going day after day in spite of road-blocks and detours? Would you invest in the best tools and equipment you could find for the trip? Would you ask the advice of people who had made the trip? Would you do your homework? I mean really do your homework!

The process of finding gold is quite different today. As the Gatlin Brothers song says: "All the gold in California is in the bank in the middle of Beverly Hills in somebody else's name."

However, to get your gold still requires the same do-or-die definite decision. It still requires tools and skills specially honed for the job. Today's gold is in the service you give your customers. The more and better service you deliver the more gold you will end up with.

Why so many fail

The odds are against you - you may not make it.

Why do so many people come into selling and after a year or two they are gone? Why do sales people fail?

Here are the reasons that sound good. These reasons justify, in the failures mind, the decision that selling is not for them. These reasons justify their failure.

"This is not worth it."

"There must be a better way to make a living."

"I'm going back to school and get a real job."

"All the good territories are already taken."

"The competition is ruthless."

"I'm going to try selling a different line."

"They expect too much."

"How can they expect me to sell anything at these prices?"

The light at the end of the tunnel went out for these "would-be" sales people. They sold themselves on the idea that they were not "cut out to be in sales."

They saw only the glamour of being independent with opportunity to earn "easy" money. Do any of these reasons sound familiar? Yes- of course they do. We have all had these thoughts at some point.

So why does one person become an outstanding success at selling while another, with the same potential, fail?

You are parked behind a restaurant sitting in your car waiting for your appointment time. You could be selling them anything. Insurance, association membership, equipment, software, food, etc. The person you are going to see is probably much older and more experienced than you. He is more than likely going to ask you something about your product line that you can't answer or don't know. As you are waiting, the anxiety grows. It is the middle of summer and the August sun is beating down on the pavement. As you get out of the car the heat and humidity are so thick you can cut it with a knife.

You walk past the dumpster and the smell practically makes you sick. As you open the door the heat from the kitchen hits you like a blast furnace. The person you are going to talk to is busy working. You know he sees you but he does not make eye contact with you. He is making you stand there as if you are invisible. At this moment in time the truth will reveal itself – are you, or are you not, going to succeed in a business with such a high failure rate? At this moment you will know how well you understand the principles and psychology of the buyer/seller relationship, or simply "The Principles of Selling."

If you DO NOT understand the PRINCIPLES your reaction is predictable. You get humiliated. Upset. Embarrassed. Mad. You take the prospects rudeness as a personal insult.

Your ego gets wounded and your mind starts filling up with negative thoughts. When he finally turns to talk to you, your attitude is reflected in your face. You try to get control of your attitude – but it's too late. The prospect won in the first round!

If you DO understand the PRINCIPLES your reaction is also predictable. You understand that you are a sales person and the prospect is on the defensive. They are afraid you are going talk them into something they do not want.

They are afraid you have a certain power over them and that is why they are ignoring you. By understanding the PRINCIPLES you know that the customer is simply setting the stage and sending you a message – a message that says he is important, his time is valuable, he is in control of this meeting. By understanding the PRINCIPLES you do not let the situation turn negative.

You say to yourself "I really love what I do – I love my profession."

"I really love playing the selling game."

"He's made his first move and he is doing it quite well."

"When he does acknowledge me I will greet him with a smile and an attitude of appreciation for letting me talk to him."

Do you see the difference? So, what is the reason so many sales people fail? Here is the reason – read it carefully.

The person who fails usually has been thoroughly trained in the products and services they are going to sell - they have NOT been trained in the psychology and principles of selling.

Sounds simple, I know.

Most non-selling managers and business owners believe that successful sales people are born that way. This is simply not true. A sales person needs professional training just as much as a doctor, lawyer, airline pilot, accountant, carpenter or chef. Why should selling be any different?

Successful sales people learn the principles of selling and apply them. Sales people who fail do not learn the principles of selling and rely on their ability to "wing it", which ultimately lets them down. We have already touched on an important principle.

ATTITUDE MANAGEMENT.

Not just having a positive attitude – but managing your attitude under all the various selling situations. Programming your mind to react in a certain way in a specific situation. It does no good to read about something as important as attitude management and then do nothing about it.

To manage your attitude you must monitor your thoughts and feelings under every selling situation. Approach it as if you were doing a scientific study. When you find that you are reacting negatively to a specific situation, you have found an opportunity to sharpen your skill.

Review your success

A class of high school basketball players with similar skills were divided into three groups to conduct an experiment.

Group one was told not to practice shooting free throws for one month.

Group two was told to practice shooting free throws an hour a day for a month.

Group three was told to practice shooting free throws an hour a day for a month - but only in their imaginations.

At the end of the month, all three groups were tested. The group that didn't practice slipped slightly in its percentage of free throw successes. The group that practiced an hour a day stayed the same. But the third group, which practiced only in their minds, increased their success rate by two percentage points. How could actual practice, such as that done by the second group, fail to improve performances as much as practicing in the mind?

The explanation is that in your mind, you never miss a shot.

What if... you did the same thing the basketball players did with the sales calls you have lined up for tomorrow?

What if... you took three minutes before turning in for the night and pictured each prospect welcoming you with open arms?

What if... you mentally reviewed everything you did RIGHT during the day rather than the mistakes you inevitably made?

Would it make a difference? You bet it would!

Several years ago, I was asked to do some sales training for a company that sold food plans. The first thing I did was go through their complete sales training program to see what they were teaching. Everything seemed perfect except for one thing.

Everyone in the training class was told repeatedly they should expect to expect to make two sales per week. Here's what I did. I had the next class of trainees told that they should expect to make 4 sales per week. All other aspects of the training were identical for both classes.

After their first month in the field, the second group had outsold the first group by a ratio of nearly two to one. Were they luckier? Was the second group getting all the breaks while the first group was having a run of bad luck?

No. The second class saw in their mind making four sales a week.

Corporations study their most profitable products. Profits permit companies to grow, in much the same way your successes challenge you to grow. The companies that grow the most have focused and improved on what they have done successfully. Did they do it by concentrating on their least profitable products or services? Do they constantly review their mistakes repeatedly?
No.

They increase their profits by concentrating on the products and services producing the most profit.

What does this mean to your selling success?

It means that your opportunities can be limitless, if you concentrate on your success rather than your mistakes. That doesn't mean you stop making mistakes. It means you change your attitude toward mistakes.

Instead of saying "If only I had done it this way or said something different," you view the mistake for what it is, something that didn't work. The key is to become well acquainted with your successes. What you are looking for are the things you are doing right.

Successful companies spend HUGE amounts of money each year in advertising to proclaim the merits of their products and services. You hold the key to your own selling success, and it can only be found in your individual performance. These nuggets are like the successful products and services the corporations concentrate on to produce the most profit.

Let's look at it from another perspective. Suppose you know two different people. One seems to fail at whatever they attempt. The other is very successful and does exceptionally well in your specific area of sales. Whose experience should you study to benefit most: the repeated failure, or the success? Whose secret would you rather know?

Successful salespeople make plenty of mistakes; however they relive and build on their achievements and successes resulting in higher and higher expectations. You will never be free of mistakes nor can you become successful by simply trying to avoid mistakes. You will continue to have many successes and many failures.

If corporations can increase their profits by identifying their greatest "pay-off" products and services, you can increase your sales by reliving your successful sales calls.

At the end of every sales call you have a choice. You can be upset or discouraged by your mistakes or you can be excited and proud of the things you did right. Even if you did not make the sale you still did several things right. By reviewing your successes, you strengthen them and give a better performance on your next call.

Try this: At you next sales meeting have 4 or 5 salespeople describe their most successful sales call.

Goal setting – what's the point?

What is the one thing that keeps you from making sales, keeps you worrying about business, and keeps you feeling insecure?

I am going to identify it but first, let me assure you, everyone is affected by it. Regardless of how long you have been in sales or how many setbacks you have to face.

Here is the hardest thing you have to do. You have to see in your mind not the way things are, but the way things can become.

This is easy to do when things are going along smooth. When customers are buying, progress is being made and things are looking pretty good. When you are in the "success frame of mind" it is easy to see all the possibilities. However, when you are up against tough times is when you are tested. That is when you really find out how difficult it is to see things the way you want them to become. Especially when you look around and you are in a seemingly impossible situation.

The law of nature insists that you grow. When you are growing and improving you are naturally positive and excited about what you are doing. However, when you run into an obstacle and you go backwards, just the opposite takes place. All of a sudden you see yourself filled with apprehension and failure.

Let's see how good of a salesperson you really are. Let's see if you can make a sale to yourself. Let's see if you can design and present a program to yourself that will get you excited about sales in spite of what everyone is saying about the economy.

Here is a common mistake most people make when they lay out a program for themselves, which you may be guilty of as well. You have been focusing on the FEATURES when you set your goals. The FEATURES are boring. The FEATURES will never get you excited. You have to give yourself a BENEFIT presentation!

In case you are not clear on the difference between a FEATURE and a BENEFIT, a feature is a fact about the product or service, a benefit is what it does.

For example, the feature of a Ford Truck is that it has a V10 450 horsepower engine. The benefit is that it will pull a 10,000-pound trailer up a steep hill with ease. The

BENEFIT is SEEING yourself driving the truck and pulling your RV or boat up the hill without any trouble.

Personal goal setting is important. What is even more important are the BENEFITS you will personally receive once your objectives are reached.

Here's what I mean. Owning your home free and clear is not a goal, but a benefit of reaching your sales and commission objective.

The extra money you want to put in your retirement account is not a goal, it is the benefit of reaching your sales objective.

Paying off your credit cards is not a goal, but a benefit of reaching your sales objective.

You talk to your customers about the benefits of your products and services - why not make the same case for selling yourself on your own personal success? Why do you want to be successful?

Lack of goal setting is rarely a problem. You either set them yourself, or your company sets them for you. Goals in themselves rarely have enough power to motivate you.

What will motivate you are the personal BENEFITS you get from accomplishing your goal. Your goal as a sales person is simple: Exceed your sales plan. If you have identified the BENEFITS you really want badly enough to take action you will be motivated. If you have not clearly identified your benefits you will not be motivated.

Exceeding your sales plan is a FEATURE not a BENEFIT. What are benefits you receive when you exceed your sales objective?

Once the benefits are listed, you will have your "reason why." You will find the personal motivation that gets you out the door early. The motivation to overcome call reluctance. The motivation to make the extra call. The motivation to ask for the additional business.

Your single goal is to exceed your sales plan. Stop now. Take out a piece of paper. Make a list of the BENEFITS you will enjoy by exceeding your sales plan. List all the BENEFITS you will receive once you exceed this goal. Better yet, get some pictures that represent the benefits and picture yourself as already having achieved them.

Growth is the purpose of life. If you are not growing, you are simply taking up space. To make progress you have to grow until you become larger than your current situation.

This attitude of GROWTH in a sales person is imperative. You MUST have it. You MUST want more. You MUST be aggressive with your actions and demand a lot from yourself. You must be able to "see" things the way they can become, not the way they are.

This is the key of a motivated sales person. A believer. A person who knows what they want. A person who is willing to pay the price. A person who has a "reason why."

Fork in the road

"Your prices are too high!"

What can you say? How do you respond?

Here's something very visual that is easy to remember and easy to use with your customers. I think it is an excellent response that you might be able to use TODAY.

Here's how it works.

When a customer says your prices are too high here's what you say:

"Joe, I can appreciate you saying that. It's true, our prices are slightly higher than some of my competitors, however, here's why. We came to a fork in the road where, as a company, we had to make a decision. We had to decide if we were going to sell on quality and service, or we were going to sell on price. We chose to sell on quality and service, and we have never been sorry."

"You can always buy something cheaper, Joe. We both know that. But my job is to help your business grow and be successful. If I sell you inferior products based on price alone, I am not helping you, I am actually hurting you."

"You are at that same fork in the road, Joe. Stick with the quality and service and you will never go wrong. Now, let's talk about these new ideas I have about how you can bring in some new customers."

Let's try it on YOU.

You are also at a fork in the road right now.

You can decide to go forward in a positive, aggressive state of mind. You can clear your mind and give it everything you've got even if things seem hopeless at the moment. You can decide to make the "do or die" commitment. You can decide that the only thing you really have control over is the action you are taking right now, knowing that if you act positive and successful your feeling will follow.

Or, you can decide to give in to the insecurity, the fear, the doubt, the wondering why you ever thought you could be successful in this career.

Choose to go forward in a positive, aggressive state of mind and you will never be sorry. Choose to let your fear and doubt take over and you will regret it the rest of your life.

Customers aren't buying

Are you running out of reasons to explain why customers are not buying and your sales are down? If your answer is yes perhaps you can find a new reason in this list.

1. What makes you any different?
2. I really don't think much of your company.
3. We've been doing all right without you.
4. I'm tied up in a supplier contract.
5. You don't carry the items I need.
6. I'm not interested in anything new.
7. See me in a couple of months.
8. I hear your company is having problems.
9. I am not talking to anyone right now.
10. Your prices have always been too high.
11. Business is down.
12. I have to run that by the owner.
13. I don't care about anything but price.
14. It would be too much work to change suppliers.

15. I don't want to jeopardize my supplier relationship.
16. If I changed suppliers why would I be any better off?
17. I'm too busy to talk to you right now.
18. I'm buying from a friend.

That list is enough to make anyone quit! On this morning's news I saw a video of a young guy quitting his job and to make it into a big event he delivered his resignation with a band playing and following him out the door. I guess if you are going to quit you might as well add a little drama. However, if you quit in sales and someone else comes along and does well where you failed, it only verifies your incompetence in the first place. I get more "drama" out of the person who doesn't quit. A person who gets up every day with that he or she can go out and make a difference in someone's business.

"Customers aren't buying" is a common complaint heard at sales meetings. The problem is, customers ARE buying, they are just not buying from you!

Even when a prospective customer gives you one of these reasons for not going forward, they still WANT to buy from you. Here's why they don't; you have not put any points on their scoreboard. Every customer has a scoreboard with points justifying their reasons for buying from their current vendor.

Who is your biggest competitor in this account? If they have been selling this customer for any length of time, they have put dozens of points on the board. They helped the customer out during a problem, they have built a personal relationship with them, they have brought new items to look at, they have given helpful information about their business, they have given them fair pricing, they have never taken advantage of their friendship, etc.

And in walks you. Zero points. And you conclude that customers aren't buying.

You can overcome all of the above 18 objections, but not with cleaver words or persuasive phrases. You can overcome them by starting today to get some points on your side of the board.

If you compare sales to a sporting event, the winner is the one who knows the rules of the game and then plays better than their competition. They learn, practice, work, put together irresistible offers and take action. They also get the extra coaching and training to make the scoreboard light up with those exciting winning numbers. They know how to make customers WANT to buy! They don't quit.

Tough time for a new rep

Is this a tough time to be a new sales rep? Maybe not! Maybe it's the best time! Just think of the freedom a brand new sales person would have!

What kind of freedom? Freedom from all the old habits that are so hard to change. Freedom from the "way we used to do it!" Freedom from the "good old days" when everybody was buying without resistance. Freedom from spending all their time complaining about the economy. Freedom from griping about how the company can't get it right. Freedom from fighting with management. Freedom from being over confident resulting in a false sense of security. They have freedom from the preconceived limitations that are found in most of the established territories.

A brand-new salesperson doesn't know that you have to work twice as hard to make the same sales as we did a few years ago. They just figure that putting in a 60-hour week is what it takes. A brand new sales person wouldn't be seeing all the limitations, they would be seeing all the opportunity, the possibilities and the chance to be of real service to their customers.

Give me an hour with a brand new sales person and I will have them so excited about selling they will be like a race horse at the gate waiting for the bell to go off. They have a clean slate. They don't have to be un-trained before they can be re-trained.

They would also have freedom from boredom, worry and fear. These negative feelings would be replaced with enthusiasm, excitement and positive expectations about the future.

A new sales person would have freedom from the dread of "yet, another sales meeting." Instead they would be excited about what they were going to learn. They would be full of curiosity, filled with questions and hungry for new ideas they could take to their customers. You remember the feeling, don't you?

A few years ago, I was asked to come in and evaluate a sales training program a company was conducting. The training was an entire week long, yet their sales were flat. At the end of the week I felt the training was excellent. The only problem was the instructor kept saying that if you make 2 sales per week you will do fine. I suggested that they make one change. Replace the "2 sales a week" to "4 sales a week" and see what happens. You guessed it. The new sales people were outperforming their old ones by 2 to 1! That's the power of freedom from previous knowledge and experience. Freedom from the power of suggestion. Like the news you watch and the gripe sessions you overhear. Block them out. Don't listen. Don't participate.

And if you are the one conducting the gripe session here's some advice for you. Here's what your colleagues are too polite to tell you. If you can't stand the heat, get out of the kitchen. Don't bring everybody else down along with you! There's a long line of eager applicants ready and willing to take your place. Be part of the solution, not the problem.

I'm not suggesting that you replace all your sales people and hire new ones. Or that you should be replaced with a new sales person. I am suggesting that you replace all your old habits and beliefs with a new attitude. A new attitude of excitement about what you do for a living. The excitement you had when you first started selling. Stop lamenting about the bad economy. This is it. This is the way it is and the way it is going to stay. So adjust. Get with the new program. Appreciate the job you have and give it everything you've got. Show yourself, your family and your company what you are really made of.

Act like today is the first day on a new exciting job!

There used to be an old saying that if you don't like selling go get a job at the post office. The post office is in trouble and getting ready to close many locations. The post office option is gone. As a matter of fact, many of the options you may have had a few years ago are gone. For whatever reason you are where you are. So step up to the plate. Stop wishing you were somewhere else doing something different and go for it.

Appreciate your job. Appreciate your customers. Appreciate the support of your family and friends. Appreciate the opportunity you have every morning to go out and help your customers. Appreciate the money you are making. Appreciate the benefits and insurance your company is providing. Appreciate your colleagues who are part of your team making the entire company successful. Nobody wants to listen to your story of defeat, doom and gloom. So stop telling it.

Remember, as a sales person or manager, your job is to solve problems. Start with your own problem, your attitude. Make it positive. Start acting like you really mean business. Put some excitement back in the way you approach your job. Pick up the pace. Start smiling again. Start acting successful. Then go and help solve your customer's problems. All it takes is one person to get it started. And little by little, the positive attitude, positive ideas, the excitement will spread and solve the huge problem of the economy. All it takes is one person like you!

Running Scared

To grow your sales and profits takes a determined, aggressive attitude. Selling in today's environment or ANY environment is not for the person who is only half decided that they are going to be the best.

Don't wait until it's too late and your customers are under attack from your competitors.

General Douglas McCarthy, US Army, knew the cause of failure in two words: "The history of failure in war can be summed up in two words: too late. Too late in comprehending the deadly purpose of a potential enemy; too late in realizing the mortal danger; too late in preparedness; too late in uniting all possible forces for resistance; too late in training our troops."

NOW is the time to make sure you are ready for battle. NOW is the time to be motivated and hungry. NOW is the time to aggressively go after new business.

There are two kinds of animals in the jungle just as there are two kinds of sales people on the street! HUNTERS and SCAVENGERS. HUNTERS keep their skills SHARP. SCAVENGERS live on the sales left over from their competitors!

I hope your area or district doesn't come under attack from someone who is a HUNTER, a person who goes after what they want.

General George Patton, US Army, knew the attitude of a HUNTER when he said: "It is the cold glitter in the attacker's eye not the point of the questing bayonet that breaks the line."

Do you have the "cold glitter" in your eye? Are you determined to have the best year ever for yourself and your family? Have you taken the oath to "Do or Die" in your sales territory? Have you taken the oath to not only maintain but to advance, to capture new accounts and to grow your sales?

You might be complaining that it is hard or difficult when customers are not buying. Here's what Admiral Ernest J King, US Navy, had to say about that: "DIFFICULTIES is the name given to things which it is our business to overcome."

You might be complaining that you have been given an impossible task.

Here's what Field Marshal Arthur Wellesley, British Army, has to say: "He who in war fails to do what he undertakes, may always plead the accidents which invariably attend military affairs: but he who declares a thing to be impossible, which is subsequently accomplished, registers his own incapacity."

If I were your competitor I would go after your small to middle size customers that you are taking for granted. The customers who pay their bills on time. The customers that you don't tell how much you appreciate. The accounts that you THINK you have sowed up. I would give them the attention and appreciation you never gave them. I would send them the cards, gifts and samples that you never thought were important. I would know everything about them.

"In war nothing is achieved except by calculation. Everything that is not soundly planned in its details yields no result."

Napoleon Bonaparte, French Emperor

Why not take the advice of these powerful military minds to plan and execute your sales strategy? Why not aggressively go after more sales, more profits and new customers?

Attitude: Define what you want and go after it

Being aggressive means moving towards what I want with the Right Mental Attitude and taking for granted that I will get it. I have a clearly defined objective and I am automatically moving toward it. Any problems or obstacles I encounter are welcomed as opportunities. They will not stop me; they only mean I have to work harder. If I make mistakes, I face up to them and correct my course of action. I am never bothered by what anyone says because they do not have all the facts and are speaking on impulse. I never allow myself to be intimidated or taken advantage of. I have a huge amount of knowledge and experience and do not have to take a back seat to anyone. Being aggressive and going after what I want will assure me of developing my sales ability to its full potential.

My 4% improvement objective:

_____

_____

_____

_____

_____

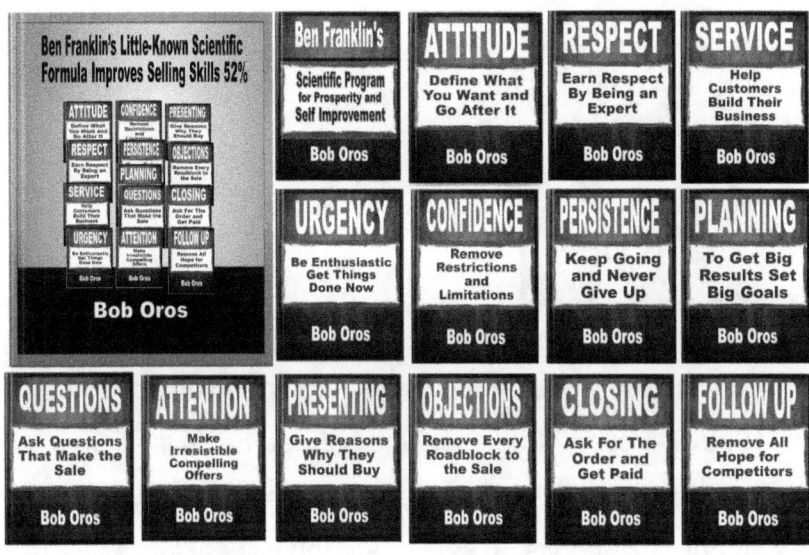

About the author Bob Oros (BobOros.com),

Bob Oros has been a full-time speaker and author since 1992 with over 2,000 speaking engagements in all 50 states and several international locations as well as the author of 21 books on sales. All Bob's speaking engagements were sold using personal selling and writing skills. Prior to starting his speaking career, Bob served six years in the US Navy as a Communications Specialist and then worked his way from a street sales person to the position of National Sales Manager for a Fortune 200 company.

CSP Award: Bob was awarded the designation of Certified Speaking Professional (CSP) by the National Speakers Association and the International Federation for Professional Speakers. Fewer than 10% of all speakers worldwide qualify for this award.

Professional Writer: As a past member of the Professional Writers Alliance along with his 35 years of sales experience, Bob writes his books and training programs in a way that will have your team members leaning forward asking for more

www.ingramcontent.com/pod-product-compliance
Lightning Source LLC
Chambersburg PA
CBHW072252170526
45158CB00003BA/1061